JOSEPH
STALIN
DICTATOR OF THE SOVIET UNION

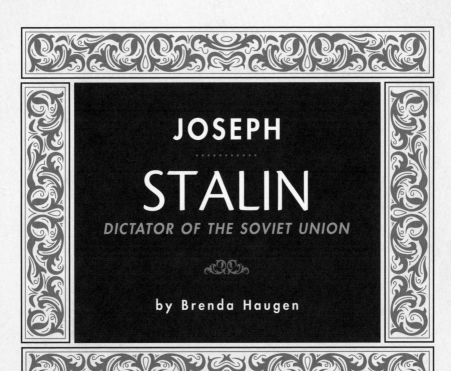

JOSEPH
STALIN
DICTATOR OF THE SOVIET UNION

by Brenda Haugen

Content Adviser: Stephen Feinstein, Ph.D.,
Director of the Center for Holocaust
and Genocide Studies,
University of Minnesota

Reading Adviser: Rosemary G. Palmer, Ph.D.,
Department of Literacy, College of Education,
Boise State University

COMPASS POINT BOOKS MINNEAPOLIS, MINNESOTA

Compass Point Books
3109 West 50th Street, #115
Minneapolis, MN 55410

Visit Compass Point Books on the Internet at *www.compasspointbooks.com*
or e-mail your request to *custserv@compasspointbooks.com*

Editor: Shelly Lyons
Page Production: Noumenon Creative
Photo Researcher: Svetlana Zhurkin
Cartographer: XNR Productions, Inc.
Library Consultant: Kathleen Baxter

Art Director: Jaime Martens
Creative Director: Keith Griffin
Editorial Director: Carol Jones
Managing Editor: Catherine Neitge

*To Joy Kundert. I don't remember a time when I didn't know you,
and I'm thankful for that fact every single day of my life. BLH*

Library of Congress Cataloging-in-Publication Data
Haugen, Brenda.
  Joseph Stalin : dictator of the Soviet Union / by Brenda Haugen.
    p. cm.—(Signature lives)
  Includes bibliographical references and index.
  ISBN 0-7565-1597-1 (hard cover)
  1. Stalin, Joseph, 1879-1953—Juvenile literature. 2. Soviet Union—
History—1925-1953—Juvenile literature. 3. Heads of state—Soviet
Union—Biography—Juvenile literature. I. Title. II. Series.
  DK268.S8H38 2006
  947.084'2092—dc22   2005025211

MODERN WORLD

From 1900 to the present day, humanity and the world have undergone major changes. New political ideas resulted in worldwide wars. Fascism and communism divided some countries, and democracy brought others together. Drastic shifts in theories and practice tested the standards of personal freedoms and religious conventions as well as science, technology, and industry. These changes have created a need for world policies and an understanding of international relations. The new mind-set of the modern world includes a focus on humanitarianism and the belief that a global economy has made the world a more connected place.

Joseph Stalin

Table of Contents

1 A RUTHLESS DICTATOR

ᕭᕮᕭ

As Soviet troops battled to protect their homeland early in World War II, Joseph Stalin, dictator of the Soviet Union, expected them to fight the Germans with every ounce of their courage and strength. Much like the German dictator Adolf Hitler, Stalin allowed no retreat and no surrender. In fact, no Soviet soldier was even expected to be captured. Some believe that he indirectly ordered troops to commit suicide rather than allow the Germans to take them as prisoners.

Stalin's son Yakov knew this. As an artillery lieutenant in the 14th Howitzer Regiment of the 14th Armored Division, Yakov refused to withdraw when German forces overran his men near Smolensk. "I am Stalin's son and I won't allow my battery to retreat," Yakov said.

Joseph Stalin rose to power in the Soviet Union by 1928 and proved to be a vicious dictator.

In 1941, Stalin's son Yakov Dzhugashvili was captured by the Germans and interrogated.

However, he was battling a lost cause. Yakov was captured. Stalin found out about it when he received a package from the Germans that included a picture of his son. "The fool—he couldn't even shoot himself!" an angry Stalin complained to his younger son, Vasily.

German authorities proposed a trade. They expected the Soviet leader would welcome his son's return. A message was sent to Stalin that said the Germans would release Yakov if the Soviets freed a German officer. Stalin refused. "I cannot do it," Stalin said. "War is war."

This decision would cost Yakov his life. Some historians believe the Germans killed Yakov, but others think he committed suicide. According to the official report, Yakov died in April 1943, after running into an electric fence surrounding the camp where he was held. Apparently Stalin never felt any remorse regarding his son's capture and death. "I have no son named Yakov," he was reported as saying after Yakov's capture.

In times of war, most leaders would find it difficult to justify offering special treatment to their own children. How could they spare their own children's lives while others died fighting for the same cause? But Stalin was different than other leaders of his time. Not only did he refuse to provide special treatment to his family, he also didn't value human life.

Stalin used his citizens as renewable natural resources. If one person died, there would always be another to replace him or her. His heartless attitude toward human beings extended to his own family.

Stalin never showed remorse

Georgia is a country located in the southwestern corner of what once was the Soviet Union. During communist rule, it was a Soviet Socialist Republic. Even though Georgia is near Russia, Georgian language differs from Russian language. Stalin's nickname in Georgian was "Soso," which means Joe in English. Stalin's mother and first wife were named Yekaterina, but in Georgian, Yekaterina is Ketevan.

Joseph Stalin threw farmers off their land and forced some to work in factories, as a part of his plan to turn the Soviet Union into an industrialized nation.

for any of the peasants he killed. Millions were murdered, jailed, or exiled as Stalin worked to make the Soviet Union a superpower. Through a series of five-year plans, he raised the Soviet Union from a struggling country with an economy based almost entirely on peasant farms, to an industrialized nation that rivaled the United States and European powers. Peasants were thrown off their small farms, and their equipment and livestock were confiscated. It all was part of the plan to collectivize farming in the country and make the process more efficient.

The cost, however, was high. Those who dared oppose his plans paid with their lives. But the death and destruction didn't stop there. As he grew more powerful, Stalin also became more fearful of losing his power. Even those closest to him faced execution or exile if he felt they posed a threat to his leadership. No one was safe in Stalin's Soviet Union. ஒ

2 AN UNHAPPY CHILDHOOD

❧❧❧

Yekaterina Dzhugashvili prayed her son, Joseph, would live. Already she'd lost two children as babies. She didn't want to lose another.

Joseph Vissarionovich Dzhugashvili, the man who would become Joseph Stalin, was born December 6, 1878, in the Georgian village of Gori. His mother, a very religious woman, named him after St. Joseph.

The Dzhugashvili family lived in a two-room shack. From their home, they could see the beautiful mountains of the Caucasus. But in Gori there was much poverty. Disease and death were always a part of their lives.

Joseph's mother prayed her son would become a priest. She tried to make Joseph feel special, by doting on him and showering him with affection, but

In 1910, Stalin changed his name from Joseph Vissarionovich Dzhugashvili to Joseph Stalin. His new last name meant "man of steel." Many Russian revolutionaries changed their names to cloak their identities. Vladimir Ilyich Ulyanov later changed his name to Vladimir Ilyich Lenin.

she was also a strict mother. Despite her religious beliefs, Yekaterina didn't hesitate to beat her son if he behaved badly. But his mother's beatings were nothing compared to those Joseph received from his father, Vissarion. An alcoholic and a shoemaker who barely earned enough to support his family, Vissarion's fiery temper could erupt at any time.

Vissarion may have been jealous of the attention that his wife gave to Joseph. He wanted his son to follow in his footsteps as a shoemaker, but his wife had other plans for Joseph. Vissarion's temper was short and his beatings were brutal.

As a boy, Joseph suffered a serious injury that stunted the growth of his left arm. Accounts of how this injury happened vary. Some historians believe it was the result of a beating from his father. Others say it happened in a carriage accident. In any case, Joseph's right arm would grow normally, but his left would be a few inches shorter.

Yekaterina didn't escape Vissarion's beatings either. Joseph felt protective toward his mother. Even as a young boy, he stood up to defend her. Once, when his father was hurting his mother, Joseph grabbed a knife and hurled it at his father to make him stop. When the knife missed its mark, Joseph rightly feared for his own life. He ran away to live with a neighbor until things in his own household cooled down.

Eventually, Joseph's mother decided they'd suffered enough abuse, and she kicked Vissarion out. He moved to the Georgian capital of Tiflis, about 30 miles (48 kilometers) from Gori. He forced Joseph to join him and work as a shoemaker's apprentice. But Yekaterina wouldn't give up her only child without a fight. With the help of priests, she retrieved her son and brought him home to live with her.

Life would remain difficult for Joseph and his mother. Yekaterina worked hard, taking in other people's laundry, to ensure their survival. At age 7, Joseph contracted smallpox. Though he recovered, his face would be scarred from the disease for the rest of his life.

In 1888, Joseph started his education at the Gori Church School, where he proved to be a good student.

Joseph Vissarionovich Dzhugashvili started school in Gori and then became a student at the Tiflis Theological Seminary in 1894, at the age of 16.

17

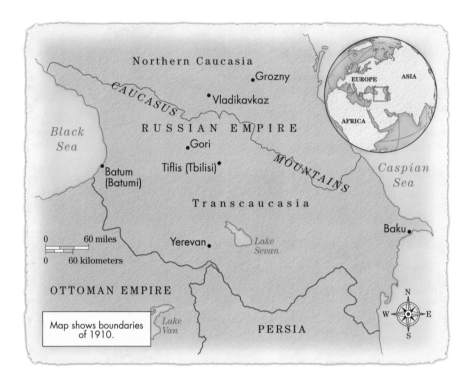

Stalin spent most of his early years in the Caucasus region of Russia.

He also discovered a flair for poetry. His first poems were romantic, but as time passed, his work became darker and more violent.

In 1894, he earned a scholarship to study at the Tiflis Theological Seminary. Yekaterina still hoped her son would become a priest, but Joseph had little interest in religion, and would never forgive his mother for sending him away from home.

At the seminary, Joseph's life revolved around classes, prayer, and homework. However, it didn't take long for him to find other interests. The strict rules of the seminary caused many students to feel angry. Some students rebelled, and Joseph was one of them. Often, they would visit stores in the city to find books the seminary had banned. The books gave them an education of the world beyond the seminary. With this knowledge, they could form their own opinions.

Joseph started forming his own beliefs about religion and government. He also started making plans for his future, and they didn't involve becoming a priest. ♔

Yekaterina Dzhugashvili died in 1937, after many years of separation from her son.

3 REVOLUTIONARY

❧❧❧

As a student in Tiflis, Stalin began reading books that were forbidden by the Russian government. Among them was a book by Karl Marx called *The Communist Manifesto*, which explained a theory called communism. Under a communist system, Marx theorized that all property used for economic production would be owned collectively by the public and would provide economic security for everyone. Marx envisioned the conversion to communism with a violent revolution, led by the workers and their representatives, the Communist Party. The working class would rise up against the middle class and take control.

In the path toward communism, the country would first move through a stage of socialism. Within

Joseph Stalin first learned about communism while he was a student at the Tiflis Theological Seminary.

this stage, the public—through the government—would share ownership of business and industry, but individuals would still earn their own unique profits. By converting their country from socialism to communism, the workers would create a classless society, where no one would own personal property and no one would make a profit.

At the time, the state of Georgia was part of the Russian Empire, which was ruled by Tsar Nicholas II. For the tsar, any talk of democracy, socialism, or communism was a form of treason.

Tsar Nicholas II was the last tsar of Russia.

But Stalin liked Marx's ideas and decided to work to make them a reality in his homeland. Based upon Marx's beliefs of socialism, the Russian Social Democratic Labor Party was formed in 1898. Vladimir Lenin led the group. That August, Stalin joined a small group of socialists in Tiflis. While he remained a student, Stalin also became a full-time revolutionary, working secretly to overthrow the tsarist government.

Though he was never a very good speaker, Stalin was assigned the task of lecturing to small groups on Marxism. For the first time in his life, Stalin felt like he was doing what he was born to do. His background and informal way of speaking made people who came from similar backgrounds comfortable listening to him. A more polished, intellectual speaker might have turned common people away from Marx's ideas, but they found Stalin appealing. He was one of them.

That fall, Stalin returned to school, but he didn't want to be there. He started failing classes and getting into trouble. After nearly five years as a student in Tiflis, he was approaching graduation. But in June, he chose to leave before taking his tests. He would never graduate.

Stalin had no desire to return to Gori. His mother was devastated when he failed to graduate. She saw her dreams for her son disappear. Throughout the rest of his life, Stalin would rarely see his mother,

Marxist revolutionary Vladimir Ilyich Ulyanov Lenin led the Russian Social Democratic Labor Party.

though he did occasionally send her money. For the rest of her life, Yekaterina would be disappointed in her son. She had wanted him to be a priest, and no other path would ever be good enough.

After leaving school, Stalin worked as a tutor and relied on the generosity of friends and other revolutionaries. In January 1900, he got a job at the Tiflis Geophysical Observatory. The pay was low, but the job afforded him plenty of time to continue his secret revolutionary activities.

Although most of Stalin's work as a revolutionary was done in secret, he gave his first public speech on communism on the outskirts of Tiflis in 1900. The speech was part of a May Day demonstration, where people were protesting bad working conditions. The government, of course, disapproved of people calling for revolution and the overthrow of government. In March 1901, the leaders of the May Day demonstration were arrested. Authorities also raided the room where Stalin lived, but he wasn't home. Knowing he'd be arrested if he returned to his room and his job, Stalin decided to give them up. He went into hiding and became a full-time communist revolutionary.

To avoid being detected by police, Stalin wore disguises and used a variety of fake names. One of his favorites was Koba. Stalin took the name from a Robin Hood-like character in one of his favorite childhood books.

Stalin took a more active role in organizing the next May Day demonstration in 1901. The event also proved more violent. About 2,000 workers rioted and fought against police. Fourteen demonstrators were injured, and more than 50 were arrested. Stalin escaped harm and went back into hiding.

Though he was on the run from police, Stalin kept trying to bring new groups of workers to the socialist cause. While spreading his message among workers in Batum, an oil port along the Black Sea, Stalin took on a new identity. He now called himself Koba.

On April 18, 1902, police finally caught Stalin in Batum and threw him in jail. As he awaited sentencing, he spent his time reading or writing letters to friends. There would be no trial. The tsarist government simply imprisoned those it arrested until it decided what to do with them.

In November 1903, a decision was reached. Stalin was exiled to Siberia, in eastern Russia, for three years. The tsar often sent criminals to Siberia because the extreme cold made for difficult living conditions. Many were also forced to work, either building the railroad system or mining coal. But the cold, barren conditions didn't hinder Stalin's escape. On January 18, 1904, Stalin used a sled to flee. He traveled about 300 miles (480 km) to Irkutsk. He secured a fake passport and arrived back in Tiflis by mid-February.

After 1918, the Bolsheviks were referred to as communists. In 1925, the party's name was officially changed to All-Union Communist Party (Bolsheviks). In 1952 it was changed again, to the Communist Party of the Soviet Union.

The year before, the Russian Social Democratic Labor Party (RSDLP), of which Stalin had been a part, had split into two groups—the Bolsheviks (majority) and the Mensheviks (minority). After his escape in 1904, Stalin became a fugitive, but he continued his work as an underground revolutionary. He chose the path of the Bolsheviks, led by Vladimir Lenin. Stalin

believed the Bolsheviks stayed closer to Marx's belief of a violent overthrow of the government, while the Mensheviks were a softer group and allowed more compromise. Stalin had rarely been one to compromise.

Between 1902 and 1913, Stalin was arrested and sent into exile in Siberia seven times. Despite the distance from home and the harsh climates he faced, he escaped six times. His last exile, from 1913 to 1917, was the only time the government was able to keep him in Siberia. 🕊

4 A New Era

❧⦿❧

Though Stalin kept busy with his revolutionary activities and evading police, he still found time to fall in love. During the summer of 1904, he married Yekaterina Svanidze, a woman who bore the same first name as his mother. She was the sister of one of Stalin's seminary classmates and a fellow Bolshevik. Yekaterina and Joseph lived in a small home near Baku, on the eastern coast of the Caucasus mountain region in Russia. However, Joseph was a busy man, traveling to Finland, Sweden, and England. He wanted to raise funds for the revolution.

Together, Joseph and Yekaterina would have one child, a son named Yakov. However, their marriage would be short-lived. Yekaterina died of tuberculosis in 1907. Stalin told a friend at the funeral:

Bolshevik fighters posed in Petrograd, Russia, after capturing an armored vehicle from the Provisional Government in 1917.

She was the one creature who softened my heart of stone. She is dead, and with her have died my last warm feelings for humanity.

Yakov went to live with Yekaterina's family, though he'd eventually return to Moscow for school, where he would live with his father once again. Although Yakov and his father were reunited, their relationship never became strong.

Stalin continued to work hard for the Bolsheviks and quickly made a name for himself. In 1907, he helped rob a bank in Tiflis to acquire funds for the Bolsheviks. In 1912, Lenin recognized his worth by naming him to the Bolsheviks' Central Committee. Stalin also began editing the Communist Party newspaper, *Pravda*.

Throughout the early 1900s, Russia was in a state of turmoil. For many years there had been a large gap between the wealthy and the poor, and Russian citizens were growing tired of it. Many Western nations were making advances in industry, which meant the gap between their wealthy and poor citizens was diminishing. Russia, however, made no such advances,

Yakov Dzhugashvili, Stalin's oldest son, became an electrical engineer and later graduated from Frunze Military Academy in Moscow. The relationship between Stalin and Yakov always remained difficult because Stalin spent so much of his time on politics. As a result, Yakov frequently rebelled in order to get his father's attention.

and this led to unrest.

In addition, Tsar Nicholas II tried to expand his empire's reach farther into China and Korea. Japan also wanted to expand its reach there. In 1904, when Japan and Russia failed to agree on expansion into China, the Russo-Japanese War erupted. The Russians lost the war in 1905 because of poor military performance. Russian citizens grew

Vyacheslav Mikhailovich Molotov (left), Stalin, and Lenin worked on Pravda, *the newspaper they founded in 1912.*

Stalin spent much of his time alone, either hunting, fishing, or reading. On occasion, he'd get a letter from his friend Olga Alliluyeva, who was to become his future mother-in-law. In at least one instance, she sent Stalin a package with food and money. He replied to her in a letter, telling her not to send money because she needed it more than he did.

> *I shall be satisfied if from time to time you send me a postcard with a view of nature and so forth. In this accursed country nature is reduced to barren ugliness—in summer the river, in winter the snow—and that's all the nature there is. I am stupidly homesick for the sight of a landscape, if only on paper.*

With the outbreak of World War I in 1914, Stalin decided not to try to escape from exile. He decided to wait for the end of the war or serve out the remainder of his sentence. However, the new Provisional Government—set up after Nicholas II gave up his throne—freed Stalin and others sent into exile by the tsar. On March 21, 1917, Stalin left for Petrograd, where he resumed work as editor of *Pravda*.

As Stalin and other Bolsheviks were being released from exile, Lenin and his top lieutenants were still out of the country. Having fled to avoid arrest, Lenin now found it difficult to return to Russia because

Vladimir Lenin often wrote articles for Pravda, *in which he voiced his own harsh opinions of Russia's Provisional Government.*

of the war. As the senior member of the Bolshevik Party now at the capital, Stalin took the opportunity to dominate the organization in Lenin's absence.

Stalin didn't impress Lenin when he appeared to compromise with Russia's Provisional Government. He also toned down Lenin's letters, which were to be printed in *Pravda*. When Lenin arrived in Petrograd in April, he immediately took back control. Although Stalin was still the editor, Lenin started to write harsh

A large crowd gathered in Red Square in 1917 to listen to Stalin and fellow revolutionary Leon Trotsky speak.

articles against the Provisional Government, but this time they weren't censored by Stalin.

On May 11, Stalin was elected to the new Central Committee of the Communist Party, a group designed by Lenin in 1912 to govern the Bolshevik Party. Stalin's work, however, was done mainly behind the scenes. He served as a liaison between the Central

Committee and Bolshevik followers in the factories, military, and the Provisional Government. While some considered Stalin to be a respected veteran of the movement, many important people close to Lenin didn't like him. And Stalin didn't go out of his way to make friends.

Meanwhile, the Provisional Government, established after the overthrow of the tsar in March 1917, and led by Alexander Kerensky, began to fall. The summer of 1917 was filled with angry protests and violence because Russia had resumed war with Germany. Increasingly, people looked to the Bolsheviks for leadership, because their position focused on ending the war as soon as possible. Membership in the Bolshevik party tripled in six months, to 240,000.

On November 7, the Bolsheviks made their move. The Red Guard, the army of industrial workers, took over important buildings in Petrograd. The Provisional Government had completely underestimated the strength of the Bolsheviks. With the fall of the Winter Palace, the place where the Provisional Government was headquartered, the Bolshevik Revolution was complete. Fewer than 12 people lost their lives that day. The trouble was far from over, though. Three years of civil war would follow.

The new Bolshevik government was approved on November 8, 1917. Stalin became one of the most powerful men in Russia. However, Lenin ranked as the undisputed leader. Stalin held an important position as head of the People's Commissariat for Nationalities' Affairs, whose main objective was to sway non-Russians into siding with the Bolsheviks. With two other strong Bolsheviks, Yakov Sverdlov and Leon Trotsky, Stalin helped Lenin make decisions on important issues in the early years of the civil war.

In March 1918, the Bolshevik government moved from Petrograd to Moscow, in order to be closer to the heartland of Russia. Stalin gained an office in the Kremlin, the ancient fortress in Moscow's center. He also made changes in his personal life. In March 1919, he married his secretary, Nadezhda Alliluyeva. The couple lived in a small house within the walls of the Kremlin.

Stalin's relationship with Trotsky was not going smoothly. Both wanted power, but Trotsky was gaining more public popularity than Stalin.

The *March 3, 1918, Treaty of Brest-Litovsk with Germany* ended World War I for Russia. In the treaty, Lenin gave up a great deal of land to Germany in order to ensure peace. Many Russians felt angry about the treaty. However, Lenin was fulfilling his pledge to get Russia out of the war and stop the killing at any price. A civil war followed, with the Reds (communists) fighting the Whites (anti-communists). Even though the Whites received support from democratic nations, the Reds were more organized and triumphed in the end.

On July 17, 1918, Tsar Nicholas II and his family were killed by Russian Bolsheviks.

As Stalin grew jealous and Trotsky became more annoyed with Stalin, Lenin tried to keep both men happy. Lenin believed both were valuable, and he didn't want them fighting each other.

On April 3, 1922, Stalin was given a new job. He was named general secretary of the Russian Communist Party. The position was important, but it involved processing a lot of paperwork from the party's day-to-day activities. No one else wanted the job. But no one knew how much power Stalin would acquire because of it. ✌

5 SEIZING POWER

ے∘⟨×⟩∘ے

By the end of 1920, the Russian civil war had ended. With the Bolsheviks in control, the Union of Soviet Socialist Republics (U.S.S.R. or Soviet Union) was formed in 1922.

As the more outgoing Trotsky worked to promote himself publicly, Stalin quietly toiled in his Kremlin office as general secretary. Stalin made use of the access his new job allowed him. At his fingertips, he had files on everyone involved in the government. He also created a network of spies to keep close watch over thousands of party officials. He wiretapped phone lines and spied on private homes. Stalin learned a great deal about everyone in the Communist Party, and he knew that someday this information would prove to be extremely valuable.

The Kremlin, which still stands in Moscow, housed the communist government from 1922 to 1991. Today it houses the Russian government.

The word kremlin comes from the Russian word for fortress. While many Russian cities have kremlins, the Kremlin is a fortress in Moscow that houses Russia's government. The Kremlin was built in 1156. Today, after numerous renovations, the Kremlin encloses 68 acres (27 hectares) of property.

That day may have come sooner than Stalin had hoped. On May 26, 1922, a blood vessel burst in Lenin's brain. Paralyzed on his right side, Lenin recovered at his country house in Gorki. Stalin visited frequently, and Lenin began to see the flaws in Stalin's personality. Lenin, who had already created a dictatorship, came to realize that Stalin coveted power for himself and cared little for his fellow party members and countrymen. Lenin wanted each of the republics that made up the Soviet Union to have a say in how they were governed. Stalin wished for an all-powerful central government to be located in Moscow. Lenin feared Stalin's dream was to create his own dictatorship.

Lenin shared his fears about Stalin with Trotsky, but their conversation didn't remain private. Stalin had wiretapped Lenin's phones, so he knew that Lenin had talked with Trotsky.

On December 16, 1922, Lenin suffered a second stroke. Knowing he wouldn't survive much longer, Lenin wrote what he called his Last Testament. In it, he detailed how he wanted the government to operate after his death. He also wrote about the most powerful government officials who would want to

succeed him after his death. This included Stalin. Lenin knew something was wrong with Stalin and wanted to warn others to keep him out of a position where he'd have too much power. Lenin wrote:

> *Comrade Stalin, having become General Secretary, has concentrated unlimited power in his hands, and I am not sure whether he always knows how to use that power with sufficient caution. ... Stalin*

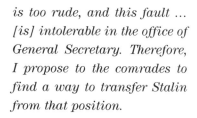

Vladimir Lenin was a dictator from the beginning of the Bolshevik Revolution, in 1917. He ruled by fear and established the Cheka, a secret police force whose goal was to find and eliminate anyone who was against the Bolshevik cause.

is too rude, and this fault ... [is] intolerable in the office of General Secretary. Therefore, I propose to the comrades to find a way to transfer Stalin from that position.

Lenin didn't make his Last Testament public right away. Instead, he put it in a drawer. Perhaps he wanted to read it at the Party Congress in April 1923. However, he never had the chance to do so. A few days before the congress met, Lenin suffered a third stroke, which left him unable to move or speak.

Stalin knew of letters Lenin dictated to his secretaries and his wife, Nadezhda Krupskaya, after he suffered his first two strokes. Since Lenin had begun to worry about the kind of person Stalin was, Stalin was concerned about what the letters might say about him. He even threatened Lenin's wife because he was afraid she would give the letters to Communist Party leaders. Stalin didn't want Krupskaya making trouble when he was so close to grabbing power for himself. "If you don't behave yourself we'll get another widow for Lenin," Stalin said menacingly to Krupskaya.

When Lenin heard about the conversation, he was enraged. His condition had improved enough that he

was able to communicate, and he sent an angry letter
to Stalin.

> *You permitted yourself a rude summons
> of my wife to the telephone and a rude
> reprimand of her. Despite the fact that
> she told you that she agreed to forget
> what was said, nevertheless Zinovyev
> and Kamenev heard about it from her. I
> have no intention to forget so easily that*

*Vladimir
Lenin's wife,
Nadezhda
Krupskaya,
helped him
with his
Communist
Party work.*

which is being done against me, and I need not stress here that I consider as directed against me that which is being done against my wife. I ask you, therefore, that you weigh carefully whether you are agreeable to retracting your words and apologizing or whether you prefer the severance of relations between us.

Lev Kamenev was a member of the Communist Central Committee.

Stalin immediately apologized.

Throughout that summer, as Lenin clung to life, Stalin scrambled for power. He formed an alliance with Lev Kamenev and Grigory Zinovyev, the two communist leaders Lenin had mentioned in his letter. Stalin believed the three of them could stand against Trotsky, whom they feared would become dictator after Lenin's death. Both Kamenev and Zinovyev believed they could control Stalin. Little did they know that Stalin would later turn on them and seize power himself.

Stalin, Kamenev, and Zinovyev began spreading rumors that Trotsky couldn't be trusted. Trotsky ignored the charges rather than defend himself,

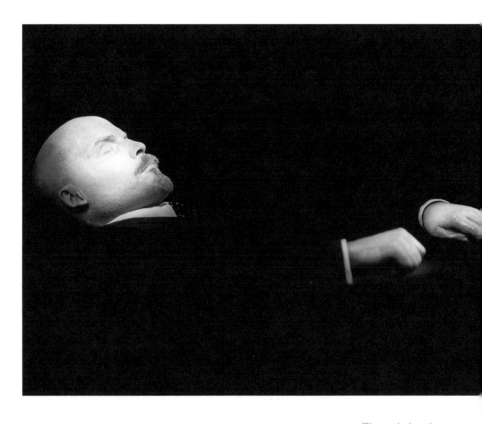

but the damage was done. It was worsened when he became sick and didn't attend Lenin's funeral on January 21, 1924. Trotsky claimed he missed the funeral because Stalin lied to him about the date, which some believe to be true.

The embalmed body of Vladimir Ilyich Lenin lies in the mausoleum in Moscow's Red Square. The body may be viewed by the public.

Stalin used Lenin's death to put himself in the spotlight. Against Nadezhda Krupskaya's wishes, Stalin ensured Lenin's funeral was a great spectacle. Stalin had Lenin's body embalmed, or preserved, and put on display in the mausoleum in Red Square. And while Stalin acted as if he had been Lenin's greatest follower, Trotsky's absence from the funeral services made him appear cold and uncaring.

Only Lenin's widow, Krupskaya, appeared to know the truth about Stalin. Despite Stalin's earlier threats, she wouldn't be silenced. When the Central Committee gathered to make plans for the future, Krupskaya read her husband's Last Testament. One witness wrote:

Grigory Zinovyev was one of Stalin's political rivals.

Terrible embarrassment paralyzed all those present. Stalin, sitting on the steps of the rostrum, looked small and miserable. I studied him closely. In spite of his self-control and show of calm, it was clearly evident that his fate was at stake.

When Krupskaya finished reading, Zinovyev rose to defend Stalin. "There is one point where, we are happy to say, Lenin's fears have proved groundless," Zinovyev said. "I am speaking on the question of our General Secretary. All of you have witnessed our harmonious cooperation during these last months, and all of you, like me, have had the satisfaction of seeing that what Lenin feared has not taken place."

The Central Committee decided to read the Last Testament privately to just a few of the congressional delegates. An angry Krupskaya threatened to have it published, but she never did. Lenin's fears about Stalin would remain a well-guarded secret until three years after Stalin's own death. Stalin was on his way to becoming the most powerful man in the Soviet Union. ℘

In 1924, Stalin used Vladimir Lenin's funeral and embalmment as a tool to promote the Communist Party. As of 2005, Lenin's embalmed body was still on display in the mausoleum in Red Square. However, some people think that his body should be removed from the mausoleum and buried.

6 THE PEASANT PURGES

❧⟨∞⟩❧

Stalin now felt free to take more control of the Communist Party and the country. By 1928, others in the party realized he was the new leader and dictator, but it was too late. Those around him grew to fear him.

Even being a member of Stalin's own family offered no protection. Though he abused his second wife, Nadezhda Alliluyeva, he may have loved her, too. At first she believed that, as Bolsheviks, she and her husband valued the same things. She even served as a spy for him. But later she would discover their morals were very different.

Alliluyeva was angry about the way Stalin was treating the millions of peasant farmers in the Soviet Union. At first, she couldn't believe the rumors she

A Soviet propaganda poster from 1934 reads: "All efforts to the gathering of the Bolshevik harvest!"

> *Stalin and his wife Nadezhda Alliluyeva differed in age. When he was 41, she was only 17. They did share some happy days together, however, and had two children—a daughter called Svetlana and a son named Vasily.*

heard, but when she confronted him, she discovered the rumors were true.

From 1924 to 1928, a series of important debates were held within the Communist Party about Russia's future. Called the Industrialization Debates, they ended with Stalin setting into motion one of his five-year plans. Because Russia had failed to pay its debt to foreign countries and banks, it had no credit and had to pay cash for anything it wished to import. Therefore, as part of the Five-Year Plan, Stalin decided to organize agriculture so that most of the grain could be exported. This was a significant change for civilians, because about 80 percent of the country was made up of peasant farms. The change would allow Stalin to make Russia an industrial power. But it would kill many of its citizens.

In 1929, Stalin, in a process called collectivization, combined more than half of the 25 million private peasant farms into collectives (shared farms) owned by the state. Those unwilling to give up their land, livestock, and other property without a fight were killed, forced into exile, or sent to labor camps, where they often literally worked themselves to death.

Still the people fought back. Some used pitchforks

A large group of farmers marched to the collective fields in a Russian village.

and axes to fight the military troops that were sent to evict them from their land. Other peasants destroyed their crops, machinery, and livestock rather than turn them over to the government. Those not punished by immediate death or exile were left to face a slow death. Stalin refused to feed the rebellious peasants. While he exported 5 million tons (4.5 million metric tons) of grain the peasants had grown, millions of these same peasants died of starvation and hundreds of thousands were sent into exile. "The peasants ate dogs, horses, rotten potatoes, the bark of trees, anything they could find," Fedor Belov, a witness to the events, wrote in December 1931.

Stalin justified his forced collectivization of farming by saying the Soviet Union needed to make advances in all areas, including agriculture, if it wanted to compete with countries such as the United States and Great Britain. To gain the money needed to import technology, Stalin took the peasants' crops for export. In 1932, he said:

> *We are fifty to one hundred years behind the advanced countries. We must catch up in ten years. Either we do it, or they crush us.*

The Communist Party used propaganda art, like posters, paintings, and movies, to gain acceptance from the public.

In time, the economy did improve, but at a tremendous price—millions of lives were lost. Millions of peasants forced off their farms were trained to work in factories or new industries established by

Stalin. Though wages were low, people had access to free medical care, low rent, and retirement funds.

As the country became more prosperous, Stalin used propaganda to turn himself into a national hero. His portrait hung in every Soviet classroom and public building. Cities, streets, factories, and other buildings were named for him.

Stalin also "touched up" his past. He made sure the Russian history books said he was involved in every major event that happened in his lifetime, whether he'd really been there or not. Anyone who dared to question the changes was either executed or exiled.

In addition, Stalin banned church services and religious books of all kinds. His position on religion was similar to Marx's: They both believed that religion was like a drug to the people. Many churches were turned into movie theaters or destroyed. Artwork was limited to Stalin's vision of how things should be. He liked art that showed happy peasants and brave revolutionaries. Anything he didn't like was banned. The same rules applied to books and music.

Stalin's family life was less

In 1930, few peasants could read or write. Because an educated workforce was needed to compete with Western nations such as the United States and Great Britain, Stalin made education a priority. By the 1940s, Russian people under the age of 50 were about as well-educated as those in Western countries.

During Stalin's rule, many churches in the Soviet Union were destroyed.

important to him than his political life. For Alliluyeva and the children, life at home often went on without the presence of a husband and father. She remained one of the few people who would stand up to Stalin. She wasn't afraid to call him a cheater or a murderer.

Stalin and Alliluyeva's relationship was a rocky one. At times, they got along well, but sometimes they seemed to hate each other. She often suffered public humiliation from her husband. Like Stalin's first wife, Alliluyeva would die young. However, even today, the circumstances surrounding her death remain cloudy.

During a party in November 1932, Stalin and Alliluyeva had a fight. Stalin insulted his wife and threw bread at her to get her attention. When he cursed at her, an embarrassed and angry Alliluyeva left the party without her husband and went home. A servant found her body the next morning. She had been shot in the heart, but no one is certain whether her death was a suicide, if Stalin killed her in a battle for her gun, or if something else happened. Her children were told she died of appendicitis, and they wouldn't find out the truth until years later.

Stalin appeared to be a heartbroken man at his wife's funeral. "I'd never seen Stalin cry before, but as he stood there beside the coffin, the tears ran down his cheeks," Molotov, a leader of the Communist Party recalled.

Stalin's second wife, Nadezhda Alliluyeva, and her daughter, Svetlana.

Though they hadn't always gotten along, Stalin had trusted Alliluyeva. He saw her death as a betrayal. And if his own wife could betray him, then no one could be trusted. Stalin would never be the same again. ☙

7 THE SHOW TRIALS

Stalin feared death. As he grew older, he became even less trusting than he had been before. He traveled in a bulletproof train or a car equipped with a machine gun under the seat. He also insisted that even his most loyal aides be searched. He was always afraid someone was going to assassinate him.

In reality, Stalin was the one to fear. He set out to eliminate his opponents in order to keep power for himself. Many historians believe he even secretly ordered the murder of friends, such as Sergei Kirov, who he believed were growing too powerful.

Kirov was a popular Communist Party leader in Leningrad, who could have proved to be a threat to Stalin's power. People admired him. While Stalin didn't enjoy getting out and meeting the common

Joseph Stalin (left) and Sergei Kirov were both Communist Party leaders, but only one would survive.

people, Kirov seemed to thrive on it. He was also handsome and a native of Russia.

While Kirov appeared to be loyal, Stalin didn't believe it. At one point, Kirov even came to Stalin and told him of rumors that some in the party wanted him to replace Stalin. Kirov told Stalin not to believe the rumors because they weren't true. Stalin wouldn't take the chance of them ever coming true.

On December 1, 1934, a disgruntled former civil servant named Leonid Nikolayev murdered Kirov outside his office. Most historians believe that Stalin was behind Kirov's death—that he had his own people infiltrate the Soviet police, called the NKVD, and had them plot Kirov's murder. Nikolayev was a Communist Party member and had been fired as a guard at the Leningrad party headquarters. He remained angry, so he was likely a willing pawn in the murder.

Faking concern, Stalin and other party officials traveled to Leningrad to investigate Kirov's death. Stalin used the assassination to spread the idea that a terrorist organization was working against the Soviet government. The same evening Kirov was killed, a secret order was issued giving the NKVD complete freedom to arrest and kill alleged terrorists. In reality, Stalin would use the excuse of terrorism to kill all his potential political competitors and enemies.

At Kirov's funeral, Stalin bent down toward the

coffin and kissed Kirov's forehead. "Goodbye dear friend, we'll avenge you," Stalin said, as everyone in the room cried.

Stalin made sure no links remained between him and Kirov's murder. Any member of the NKVD who knew or even wondered whether Stalin had a part in the assassination mysteriously disappeared, never to be seen again.

The Great Terror had begun. For the next 19 years, Stalin's control would be complete. No one dared to disagree with him and no one felt safe. Many citizens were accused of being against communism and the Five-Year Plan, as well as Stalin's dictatorship. Those accused didn't receive a public trial, and torture was used to gain confessions.

The Russian city Petrograd was originally named St. Petersburg. In 1914, it was renamed Petrograd, and in 1924, it was renamed Leningrad, in honor of Vladimir Lenin. However, in 1991 the city regained its original name, St. Petersburg. Stalingrad was originally called Tsaritsyn, but in 1925, it was renamed Stalingrad, in honor of Joseph Stalin. Finally, in 1961, it was stripped of its name and given the new name Volgograd.

Even the high-ranking members of the Communist Party lived in fear. They were so afraid that they refused to be the first to stop clapping for Stalin at gatherings. They didn't want to appear unfaithful or unenthusiastic. The unending clapping eventually grew to be such a problem that a bell would sound,

Stalin was a pallbearer at Kirov's funeral, in 1934. Kirov's assassination marked the beginning of the Great Terror.

letting them know when the applause should end.

With the general public, Stalin made every effort to appear as a caring, fatherly man. He welcomed opportunities to have his picture taken at ceremonies where he accepted flowers from little girls or handed out medals to patriotic Soviets. The standard of living improved, and food rationing that had been put in place in 1929, finally came to an end in 1935. Unaware that Stalin stood behind the murder of innocent citizens, the general public came to see him as a hero.

Meanwhile, Stalin admired another man coming to power in Europe—Adolf Hitler. On June 30, 1934, Hitler ordered the murders of many members of his own private army, the SA. "Did you hear what happened in Germany?" Stalin asked one of his comrades. "Some fellow that Hitler! Splendid! That's a deed of some skill!"

Stalin placed his rival Leon Trotsky at the head of the list of terrorists wanting to overthrow the Soviet government. He had Trotsky removed from the Communist Party and exiled to Turkey. Trotsky later moved to Mexico. In August 1940, after several failed attempts on Trotsky's life, Stalin finally succeeded in having Trotsky killed just outside Mexico City, Mexico.

Stalin had a similar purge in mind. Kirov's death gave him an excuse to remove hundreds of thousands of alleged enemies. On August 19, 1936, the first of the Show Trials began. These trials were aimed mainly at leaders of the Communist Party who had helped Stalin into power or knew about his methods. They were called the Show Trials because the accused had to agree to confess, as if they were reading the scripted lines of a play. The two men who had helped Stalin rise to power—Zinovyev and Kamenev—went on public trial along with 14 other Bolsheviks. Each was charged with organizing terrorist activities under Trotsky's leadership.

Those charged were threatened into confessing to crimes. Because the trials were public, the defendants weren't harmed physically—bruises and other injuries would have made citizens doubt the defendants' confessions. Instead, police threatened the lives of the defendants' loved ones. If they didn't confess, their families were to be killed. The tactic worked, and all 16 men on trial confessed that they had planned acts of terrorism against Stalin and the

Adolf Hitler was dictator of Germany from 1933 to 1945.

Soviet government. The confessions were made publicly, so no further testimony was needed. All the defendants were found guilty and shot to death.

However, this wasn't the end. In their confessions, the men were forced to name others involved in the fake conspiracy. A second Show Trial was held January 23, 1937. The results proved similar to the first trial. Four of the defendants received long prison terms, but the other 13 were executed.

If anyone felt uncomfortable with the trials in any way, they kept their mouths shut. They didn't want to be the next one put on trial.

Later that year, Stalin turned against his own military. He killed anyone he feared might hatch a plot against him. In 1937 and 1938, Stalin may have executed as many as half of his 70,000 officers. Included in this number were 90 percent of his generals and 80 percent of his colonels. The leadership of the military was almost destroyed.

Those Stalin had murdered lost not only their lives but their total existence as well. They were eliminated from public records, books, and photographs. Any traces that they ever existed were erased.

Stalin didn't attend the executions of those found guilty during the Show Trials. However, he did enjoy hearing stories about how those sentenced to death were humiliated and had begged for their lives. One witness re-enacted Zinovyev's last moments and made Stalin laugh so hard, the leader had to wave his hands for the re-enactment to stop.

The third and last of the Show Trials occurred in March 1938. Eighteen of the 21 on trial were shot to death after their confessions. Three escaped with long prison terms.

Most of those killed did nothing to deserve such a fate. Many believed their arrests were just misunderstandings and that the truth would come out. In many cases, those charged with crimes believed Stalin was blind to what was happening and that evil people working around him were respon-

sible for their misfortune. They didn't realize Stalin not only knew everything that was happening, but in fact was the mastermind of the whole purge.

Robert Eikhe was one of those accused who didn't believe Stalin knew innocent people were being murdered after confessing to crimes they didn't commit. Eikhe hoped he could open the leader's eyes. He wrote a letter to Stalin, in hopes of saving those he'd falsely accused under pressure from the police.

In 1936, workers at a mechanical shop in Russia voted for the severe punishment of those who were on trial.

I have not been guilty of even one of the things with which I am charged and my heart is clean of even the shadow of baseness. I have never in my life told you a word of falsehood and now, finding my two feet in the grave, I am also not lying. ... I am asking and begging you that you examine my case, and this not for the *purpose of sparing me but in order to unmask the vile provocation which, like a snake, wound itself around many persons in a great degree due to my meanness and criminal slander. I have never betrayed you or the party. I know that I perish because of vile and mean work of the enemies of the party and of the people, who fabricated the provocation against me.*

Eikhe was shot to death in 1940.

In Moscow alone, 1,500 to 3,000 people were shot to death each day during 1937. Stalin's victims included not only his enemies but also people innocent of any wrongdoing or personal offense toward him. While the executions didn't seem to bother him, he would soon pay a price for devastating his military.

Estimates of the death toll during Stalin's Great Terror vary widely. Some historians say at least 7 million citizens were killed immediately or died slow deaths in the Gulag, a series of labor camps that were built across the Soviet Union. Others place that number at close to 20 million. ꙮ

Chapter

8 WORLD WAR II

❧◆❧

In 1933, Adolf Hitler came to power as chancellor of Germany. He developed plans to recover land that had been stripped from his country after World War I. But his plans didn't stop there. Hitler dreamed of a vast German empire and believed it was his destiny to rule the world.

Hitler planned to attack Poland, which he knew would likely draw France and Great Britain into a war to stop Germany. But he didn't want to face a second front as well—a possible fight with the Soviet Union to the east.

Stalin didn't want war with Germany either. After purging his military, he knew he wasn't prepared to fight the Germans.

In August 1939, the Soviet Union and Germany

German Foreign Minister Joachim von Ribbentrop, Joseph Stalin, and Soviet Foreign Minister Vyacheslav Mikhailovich Molotov (seated), signed the German-Soviet nonaggression pact.

signed a nonaggression pact. The pact bought Stalin some time to build up his military again. It also divided Poland between Germany and the Soviet Union. In September, Germany invaded western Poland, marking the start of World War II. Soon after, the Soviets invaded eastern Poland. Within a year, thousands of innocent Polish citizens were killed.

Stalin also provided aid to Hitler. The Soviet Union started selling large amounts of raw materials to Germany. In addition, Stalin allowed Japan, one of Germany's allies during the war, to transport goods across the Soviet Union to Germany. While Stalin's relationship with Hitler proved profitable in the beginning, it wouldn't be long before Hitler betrayed the Soviet leader.

The front page of London's Evening Standard *newspaper on September 1, 1939, told* the public *of the German* invasion *of Poland.*

LATEST PRICES　　　　　　　　　LATE NIGHT FINAL

ITS CLEAR Nicholson's Gin ITS GOOD

Evening Standard

La Coquille

No. 35,880　　LONDON, FRIDAY, SEPTEMBER 1, 1939　　ONE PENNY

GERMANS INVADE AND BOMB POLAND BRITAIN MOBILISES

Warsaw, Cracow, Nine Other Towns Bombed: Danzig is "Annexed"

FRANCE DECLARES "STATE OF SIEGE"

In early summer of 1941, Stalin received many warnings about a German invasion of the Soviet Union, but he ignored them. He believed the warnings were rumors spread by Western countries to get the Soviet Union to join in the battle against Germany.

Stalin believed Hitler would stand by the nonaggression agreement they had signed. He also believed Hitler would never start a fight with the Soviet Union when he still faced danger from Great Britain. Fighting a war on two fronts wouldn't be a good strategy. However, that's exactly what Hitler ended up doing. Even after the warnings proved true, Stalin still couldn't believe it.

During his dictatorship, Adolf Hitler ordered the killing of 6 million Jews. His master plan included the elimination of all those who were not Aryan: Caucasian, blonde-haired, and blue-eyed. He also had thousands of others killed, including political and religious leaders, gypsies, male homosexuals, and disabled individuals.

Hitler broke the nonaggression agreement and invaded the Soviet Union on June 22, 1941. He had never planned to honor the agreement because he saw Russia as space for his country to grow. He also wanted Russian agriculture and fuel. Throughout the war, Hitler took resources from the countries he had conquered.

Three million Nazi soldiers crossed the border, invading the Soviet Union. Most of the Soviet air

Russian militia posed during the siege of Leningrad, which lasted almost 900 days.

force was destroyed as it sat on the ground. Stalin was stunned. So was the Soviet Union's Red Army. Hundreds of thousands of Soviet soldiers were killed or captured in the first days after the invasion. Equipment concentrated along the border was smashed by the German blitzkrieg, or lightning war.

Surprised and betrayed, Stalin suffered a mental breakdown. Without direction from him, the Red Army didn't know what to do. After more than a week,

Stalin finally pulled himself together. In a speech to his citizens on July 3 , he still seemed visibly shaken, but this may have worked in his favor. He appealed to his citizens' patriotism and called for the defense of their homeland. He begged them not to give up hope. The citizens responded.

The Soviets adopted a "scorched earth" policy. As the Germans made their way east, the Soviets left nothing behind. Railroad tracks, food supplies, equipment, and anything else that would aid the Germans were destroyed as the Soviets retreated.

Hitler launched an attack that stretched eastward across 930 miles (1,488 km). Within six months, about 4 million Soviet soldiers were captured. Another 3 million had been killed. Most of Ukraine was occupied by German troops. Leningrad was under attack, and Moscow was feeling threatened as German soldiers drew closer.

But Hitler underestimated the Russian military. The Russians began beating back the Germans before the end of the year. The German army was surprised by the Russian winter, which came early in 1941. Thousands of German soldiers died as a result of frigid

Leningrad was under siege from the Germans from September 1941 to January 1944. The siege caused severe shortages of food and basic supplies. The winter of 1942 was extremely difficult, because of severe cold temperatures and lack of food. About 1.5 million residents of Leningrad perished. Most died from hunger.

World War II was fought from 1939 to 1945. The Axis powers were led by Germany, Italy, and Japan. The Allied powers were led by the United States, Great Britain, and the Soviet Union.

temperatures and a lack of proper supplies.

In 1942, goods from the United States started arriving in the Soviet Union through the Lend-Lease Act. Under this new law, President Franklin Roosevelt was able to send weapons, equipment, and food to any country fighting against Germany and its allies.

In September, Stalin launched a land and air attack against the Germans in Stalingrad. Some historians believe that if any of his soldiers retreated, Stalin ordered they be shot.

In February 1943, German troops were defeated at Stalingrad and began suffering other losses along the eastern front. Though the fighting would go on for another two years, the Soviets' victory at Stalingrad proved to be the turning point in the war. After that, the siege of Leningrad was lifted and the Red Army went on the offensive, liberating Eastern Europe in 1944 and capturing Berlin in April 1945. ❧

9 THE COLD WAR BEGINS

Chapter

❧❧❦❧❧

In 1945, just before the end of World War II in Europe, the Big Three—Stalin, Roosevelt, and Great Britain's Winston Churchill—met at Yalta, at the southern tip of the Crimean Peninsula in Ukraine, to discuss how to proceed once peace was restored.

Churchill wanted a free, democratic Europe. Stalin wanted to protect his borders so he wouldn't face attack again. Roosevelt wanted to finish the war with Japan and was willing to compromise with Stalin to secure peace.

All three agreed to the establishment of a peacekeeping organization, which would later become the United Nations. They also agreed to divide Germany into three zones between the United States, England, and the Soviet Union. A French zone

Winston Churchill (left), Franklin D. Roosevelt, and Joseph Stalin met at the Yalta Conference in 1945.

He knew the country and agriculture only from films. And these films had dressed up and beautified the existing situation in agriculture. Many films so pictured kolkhoz [collective farm] life that the tables were bending from the weight of turkeys and geese. Evidently, Stalin thought that it was actually so.

Harry Truman was the 33rd president of the United States. He took over the presidency when Franklin Roosevelt died in 1945, just before World War II ended.

In March 1946, Stalin unveiled the fourth step in his Five-Year Plan: He increased oil, coal, and steel production. During this time, Stalin also dedicated Soviet resources to the development of the atomic bomb. In addition, he pulled away from any relationship he may have started with the West during World War II. In August 1945, the Lend-Lease Act ended abruptly, which meant the aid that the Soviet Union had been receiving from the United States was no longer available. This made Stalin bitter toward the United States and its allies. This bitterness between the Soviet Union and the United States started what is called the Cold War.

The Marshall Plan, which began in 1948, aided war-torn countries throughout Europe. It provided much-needed food and supplies to countries that agreed to fight against communism. The United States sent more than $10 million worth of supplies to countries in need during that time. The plan ended in 1952.

In 1947, President Harry Truman announced a plan to aid countries fighting against communism. The Marshall Plan also gave billions of dollars to noncommunist countries to help rebuild after World War II. For Stalin, this was a huge slap in the face. The Soviet Union's suffering citizens needed all the help they could get, but as a communist nation, they weren't eligible for U.S. aid. This drove the wedge between the Soviets and Americans even deeper.

Problems remained in Germany, as well. At the

end of World War II, Germany had been split into three zones. The capital city of Berlin lay within the Soviets' zone, but it also was divided into two separate zones—East and West Berlin. When the Soviet Union couldn't reach an agreement with the other three countries on how to heal Germany, the United States, Great Britain, and France decided to combine their areas and form the new country of West Germany in 1948. The Soviet Union took control of East Germany, and East Berlin.

An angry Stalin tried to force the other nations

Children in West Berlin cheered for a U.S. cargo plane bringing food and supplies.

out of West Berlin by blockading the city. He didn't allow food or any other supplies to be brought there. Although this angered the Allied nations, it didn't stop them. The city received supplies by airplane from France, Great Britain, and the United States. This effort was known as the Berlin Airlift, which lasted for nearly a year. Eventually, Stalin backed down and ended the blockade, but bad feelings between the Soviets and the Western nations remained. In time, Stalin cut off nearly all communication with the West. ✍

In 1961, the Soviets built the Berlin Wall, which divided the city of Berlin. The wall was designed to keep citizens of East Berlin from emigrating to the West. It remained in place until 1989, when the citizens of East Berlin protested. The government decided to open the wall. Today, Berlin and Germany are no longer divided.

Chapter
10 STALIN'S FINAL YEARS

◆◇◆

Stalin's personal life continued to crumble after World War II. His son Yakov died during the war, and his other son, Vasily, suffered from alcoholism. His daughter, Svetlana, married a Jew, which angered her anti-Semitic father. Stalin rarely saw her anymore. As for friends, Stalin had killed many of them in his purges. Those who remained often suffered insults from Stalin.

Toward the end of the 1940s, however, Stalin seemed to realize his own days were numbered. In 1949, he tried to secure his place in history by publishing the first 16 volumes of his *Collected Works*. In 1950, he started an ambitious building program of bridges, canals, and other projects designed to show his ability to control the natural environment.

In 1950, Joseph Stalin tried to preserve his name for generations to come by making sure Russian books, art, and photos portrayed him as a beloved leader.

However, many of the projects were never finished.

Stalin also tried to show people he was a man of peace—by having Russian history books rewritten. He wanted the books to show his history in a positive light. Despite the terror he caused, he wanted peace and prosperity to be part of his legacy. Evidence of this was heard in October 1952, during the last

A Communist Party history book was rewritten to include information on Stalin. His profile was added to the cover.

speech he'd ever give before the Communist Congress. "Long live peace among nations!" he cried. "Down with the warmongers!"

In reality, Stalin hadn't changed into a peace-loving person. In fact, may have been planning another purge. Many experts believe Stalin had plans to deport the Jewish population of the Soviet Union to the Far East.

On January 13, 1953, seven doctors were accused of plotting to kill government officials who were their patients. Throughout his life, Stalin strongly distrusted doctors. He even had his own doctor arrested as a spy.

In the early 1950s, many Jewish Soviets did not feel safe. There was an increasing belief that Stalin had intentions to deport the Soviet Jewish population to the East. Whether this is true or not remains unknown, but many experts believe that had it not been for his death, Stalin would have followed through with a purge of the Soviet Jews.

According to Stalin, the United States and Great Britain were behind the conspiracy. Five of the seven doctors arrested were Jewish. In time, hundreds of other Jews were arrested and forced to say they, too, were part of the conspiracy. As these innocent people waited in terror to see what their fate would be, their circumstances changed.

On March 1, at his country estate outside Moscow, Stalin suffered a burst blood vessel in his brain. Paralyzed and helpless, he lay on the floor for hours until guards found him.

At first, Stalin's condition was kept secret from the public. As his condition grew worse, it became obvious he wouldn't recover. On March 5, Stalin died. His daughter, Svetlana, and Communist Party faithful leaders were at his side. His death may have prevented another purge from being carried out—which saved the Jews he had charged in the imaginary conspiracy. And it proved a tortuous end for a man who had caused so many others great pain. Svetlana said:

Stalin's body was on display in Moscow.

The death agony was horrible. He literally choked to death as we watched. At what seemed like the very last moment he suddenly opened his eyes and cast a glance over everyone in the room. It was a terrible glance, insane or perhaps angry and full of the fear of death and the unfamiliar faces of the doctors bent over him. … Then something incomprehensible and awesome happened that to this day I can't forget and don't understand. He suddenly lifted his left hand as though he were pointing to something above and bringing down a curse on us all. The gesture was incomprehensible and full of menace, and no one could say to whom or at what it might be directed. The next moment, after a final effort, the spirit wrenched itself free of the flesh.

Stalin's daughter, Svetlana, defected to the United States in 1967. Shortly after, she released her memoirs, titled Twenty Letters to a Friend. She later changed her name to Lana Peters. She moved back to the Soviet Union in 1984 but remained there for only two years before she moved back to the United States. Later, she settled in England.

Stalin's body was moved to Red Square, at the center of Moscow, and remained there until the funeral took place. While many Soviet citizens mourned his death, others felt relieved he was gone.

Just as Lenin's had been, Stalin's body was embalmed. This allowed his body to be put on display.

Stalin's coffin was draped with red and black

After a struggle to gain power, Nikita Krushchev took over as premier of the Soviet Union in 1958.

silk. On March 9, hundreds of thousands of people watched as Stalin was laid to rest in the Kremlin mausoleum, next to Lenin. The crowd tried to draw closer as the funeral procession made its way through Red Square. As people pushed and shoved for better views, a riot erupted. More than 500 people were killed in the crush of the crowd.

Many men struggled for power after Stalin's death. Nikita Khrushchev finally won the leadership role. Khrushchev made improvements in the Soviet Union and even reached out to Western nations. He also made bold statements against Stalin, the man he once served under. During a 1956 Communist Party gathering, Khrushchev gave a speech in which he talked about Stalin's brutal crimes against his people. "In a whole series of cases, Stalin showed his intolerance, his brutality and his abuse of power," Khrushchev said. The speech was kept a secret from the public.

Just as the country was changing, so was Stalin's

own family. His daughter, Svetlana, decided to change her name from Svetlana Stalina, to Svetlana Alliluyeva. This was a serious step, and it proved that even Svetlana recognized the fact that the name *Stalin* would not be thought of in a positive light.

The Soviet Union fell apart in 1991, when most of the 15 republics declared their independence. Now, the former Soviet Union consists of many countries, such as Russia, Georgia, Kazakhstan, Ukraine, and others.

Stalin's reburial was also kept a secret from the Soviet public. During the Communist Party gathering in the fall of 1961, Khrushchev strongly suggested that Stalin's body be moved. Dora Abramovna Lazurkina, one of Lenin's faithful followers in the 1917 revolution, agreed. She had suffered at the hands of Stalin. Although she survived 17 years in prison and labor camps, many of her friends did not. She believed Lenin's ghost spoke to her and said he didn't like being so close to Stalin. Lazurkina told the communists at the meeting:

> *Yesterday I consulted [Lenin]. He was standing there before me as if he were alive, and he said: "It is unpleasant to be next to Stalin, who did so much harm to the party."*

In October, Stalin's body was removed from the mausoleum and reburied outside the Kremlin wall.

Even today, there are people in Russia who believe Joseph Stalin was a fair and respectful leader.

His coffin was encased in a pit filled with tons of cement, to ensure it wouldn't ever be moved again. A few weeks later, a granite slab with the inscription "J. V. Stalin" was placed on the grave.

In the years following his death, Stalin's portraits were removed from buildings, and his statues were destroyed. Stalingrad was renamed Volgograd, and the names of other cities and streets once named for him were changed as well. During his life, many saw Stalin as a hero. After his death, some Soviet citizens came to see him for what he really was—a gruesome dictator and murderer.

Russia has recently moved toward democracy. Today, much information about Stalin's rule has been released to the public. Although there are some citizens who have changed their minds about Joseph Stalin, there are also those who consider the information to be false. Those citizens remain loyal to his memory. They choose to remember only the positive things that took place under Stalin's rule, like the defeat of the German Nazi forces in World War II. They ignore the fact that he was responsible for the deaths of millions of people. ॐ

STALIN'S LIFE

1878

December 6, Joseph Stalin is born Joseph Dzhugashvili in Gori, Georgia

1888

Begins his formal education at a church school in Gori

1894

Earns a scholarship to attend the Tiflis Theological Seminary

1890

1886

Grover Cleveland dedicates the Statue of Liberty in New York, a gift from the people of France

1879

Electric lights are invented

1893

Women gain voting privileges in New Zealand, the first country to take such a step

WORLD EVENTS

1898

Becomes a
revolutionary,
joining a group
of socialists
in Tiflis

1899

Leaves the Tiflis
Theological
Seminary just
weeks before
graduation

1902

Is arrested as
a revolutionary
for the first time

1900

1896

The Olympic Games
are held for the first
time in recent history
in Athens, Greece

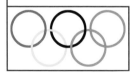

1901

Britain's Queen
Victoria dies

STALIN'S LIFE

1910

Changes
his name to
Joseph Stalin

1903

Is exiled to Siberia
for the first of seven
times; he would
escape six times

1904

Marries his first wife,
Yekaterina Svanidze,
who would die three
years later

1905

1903

Brothers Orville and
Wilbur Wright successfully
fly a powered airplane

1909

The National
Association for
the Advancement
of Colored
People (NAACP)
is founded

WORLD EVENTS

1917

At the end of
World War I,
Stalin becomes a
free man again

1919

Marries his second
wife, Nadezhda
Alliluyeva

1928

Begins first Five-
Year Plan to
industrialize the
Soviet Union

1925

1916

German-born physicist
Albert Einstein publishes
his general theory of
relativity

1919

World War I
peace conference
begins at
Versailles, France

1926

Claude Monet and
Mary Cassat, well-
known impressionist
painters, die

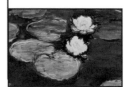

STALIN'S LIFE

1934
The Great Terror begins following the assassination of Sergei Kirov

1939
U.S.S.R. signs nonaggression agreement with Germany in August

1932
Nadezhda Alliluyeva dies under mysterious circumstances

1935

1933
Nazi leader Adolf Hitler is named chancellor of Germany

1939
German troops invade Poland; Britain and France declare war on Germany; World War II (1939–1945) begins

WORLD EVENTS

1945

Meets with Franklin Roosevelt and Winston Churchill at Yalta Conference

1953

Suffers a cerebral hemorrhage March 1 and dies March 5; reburied in October 1961

1950

1945

The United Nations is founded

1949

Birth of the People's Republic of China

1953

The first Europeans climb Mount Everest

DATE OF BIRTH: December 6, 1878, but officially celebrated as December 21, 1879

BIRTHPLACE: Gori, Georgia

FATHER: Vissarion Dzhugashvili

MOTHER: Yekaterina Dzhugashvili

EDUCATION: Gori Church School and Tiflis Theological Seminary

FIRST SPOUSE: Yekaterina Svanidze (?–1907)

DATE OF MARRIAGE: June 1904

CHILDREN: Yakov Dzhugashvili (1907–1943)

SECOND SPOUSE: Nadezhda Alliluyeva (?–1932)

DATE OF MARRIAGE: March 1919

CHILDREN: Vasily (1921–1962) Svetlana (1926–   )

DATE OF DEATH: March 5, 1953

PLACE OF BURIAL: Moscow, Russia

Further Reading

Caulkins, Janet. *Joseph Stalin*. New York: Franklin Watts, 1990.

Gottfried, Ted. *The Stalinist Empire*. Brookfield, Conn.: Twenty-First Century Books, 2002.

Marrin, Albert. *Stalin*. New York: Puffin Books, 1993.

Otfinoski, Steven. *Joseph Stalin: Russia's Last Czar*. Brookfield, Conn.: Millbrook Press, 1993.

Ross, Stewart. *The USSR Under Stalin*. New York: Bookwright Press, 1991.

Look for more Signature Lives
books about this era:

Benazir Bhutto: *Pakistani Prime Minister and Activist*
ISBN 0-7565-1578-5

Fidel Castro: *Leader of Communist Cuba*
ISBN 0-7565-1580-7

Winston Churchill: *British Soldier, Writer, Statesman*
ISBN 0-7565-1582-3

Jane Goodall: *Legendary Primatologist*
ISBN 0-7565-1590-4

Adolf Hitler: *Dictator of Nazi Germany*
ISBN 0-7565-1589-0

Queen Noor: *American-born Queen of Jordan*
ISBN 0-7565-1595-5

Eva Perón: *First Lady of Argentina*
ISBN 0-7565-1585-8

ON THE WEB

For more information on *Joseph Stalin*, use FactHound.

1. Go to *www.facthound.com*
2. Type in a search word related to this book or this book ID: 0756515971
3. Click on the *Fetch It* button.

FactHound will fetch the best Web sites for you.

HISTORIC SITES

Franklin D. Roosevelt Presidential Library
4079 Albany Post Road
Hyde Park, NY 12538
800/FDR-VISIT
Information on World War II and Franklin Roosevelt's dealings with Joseph Stalin

John Fitzgerald Kennedy Library
Columbia Point
Boston, MA 02125
617/514-1600
Information on the Cold War.

Cold War
the conflict between the United States and the U.S.S.R. that did not result in actual war

collectivize
to gather smaller things together into one big group

communist
a system in which the government owns a country's businesses and controls the economy; a person who supports communist governments

confiscated
taken something by authority

dictator
a ruler who takes complete control of a country, often unjustly

exiled
sent away or cast out

fabricated
made up

fugitive
a runaway; a person on the run from the law

incomprehensible
unable to be understood

labor camps
colonies where people are forced to perform hard labor

liaison
someone who establishes contact and understanding between two groups

mausoleum
a large building that houses tombs

pawn
a person or thing used by someone to gain
some advantage

propaganda
ideas, facts, or allegations spread deliberately
to further one's cause or to damage an
opposing cause

purge
the removal of elements or members regarded as
undesirable, treacherous, or disloyal

remorse
a strong feeling of guilt after doing
something wrong

rostrum
a stage for public speaking

siege
a military blockade of a city, to make it surrender

slander
to make false statements about someone else

socialists
followers of an economic system in which the
government owns most businesses

tsar
a Russian ruler

wiretapped
to place a device on a telephone line that
allows conversations to be heard secretly;
used to get information

Chapter 1

Page 9, line 13: Simon Sebag Montefiore. *The Court of the Red Tsar.* New York: Alfred A. Knopf, 2004, p. 379.

Page 10, line 4: Ibid.

Page 10, line 11: Thomas Fuchs. *A Concise Biography of Adolf Hitler.* New York: Berkley Books, 2000, p. 65.

Page 11, line 8: 23 Nov. 2005. http://en.wikipedia.org/wiki/Yakov_Dzhugashvili.

Chapter 4

Page 30, line 1: Steven Otfinoski. *Joseph Stalin: Russia's Last Czar.* Brookfield, Conn.: Millbrook Press, 1993, p. 35.

Page 33, line 1: Robert Warth. *Joseph Stalin.* New York: Twayne Publishers, 1969, p. 31.

Page 34, line 9: Ibid.

Chapter 5

Page 43, line 5: *Joseph Stalin: Russia's Last Czar,* p.49.

Page 44, line 25: *Joseph Stalin,* p. 46.

Page 45, line 3: Ibid., p. 48.

Page 49, line 1: Ibid., p. 52.

Page 49, line 11: *Joseph Stalin: Russia's Last Czar,* p. 53

Chapter 6.

Page 53, line 11: *The Court of the Red Tsar,* p. 82.

Page 54, line 8: *Joseph Stalin: Russia's Last Czar,* p. 58.

Page 57, line 14: *The Court of the Red Tsar,* p. 108.

Chapter 7

Page 61, line 2: Ibid., p. 155.

Page 63, line 14: Ibid., p. 131.

Page 68, line 1: *Joseph Stalin,* p. 79.

Chapter 9

Page 82, line 1: Ibid., p. 117.

Chapter 10

Page 89, line 2: *Joseph Stalin: Russia's Last Czar,* p. 103.

Page 91, line 1: Ibid., p. 104.

Page 93, line 21: Ibid., p. 10.

Fuchs, Thomas. *A Concise Biography of Adolf Hitler*. New York: Berkley Books, 2000.

Montefiore, Simon Sebag. *Stalin: The Court of the Red Tsar*. New York: Alfred A. Knopf, 2004.

Service, Robert. *Stalin: A Biography*. United Kingdom: Macmillan Publishers Ltd, 2004.

Toland, John. *Adolf Hitler, Volume II*. New York: Doubleday & Company, Inc., 1976.

Tucker, Robert C. *Stalin in Power: The Revolution From Above, 1928-1941*. New York: Norton, 1990.

Ulam, Adam B. *Stalin: The Man and His Era*. Boston: Beacon Press, 1989.

Warth, Robert D. *Joseph Stalin*. New York: Twayne Publishers, Inc., 1969.

Brenda Haugen started in the newspaper business and had a career as an award-winning journalist before finding her niche as an author. Since then, she has written and edited many books, most of them for children. A graduate of the University of North Dakota in Grand Forks, Brenda lives in North Dakota with her family.

Image Credits